IRISH TIN WHISTLE
INTROD

95P

GW01080088

Tin whistles are manufactured in differe
more commonly used. However, it is important to
tune will be the same regardless of the key in whicl
is built of solid brass with a specially designed pl:
an unmatched, clear, flute-like tone quality. Alth
there are no sharps or flats involved, I have arrange
reasons:

1. It is easier to produce good quality tones with little effort.
2. It is not necessary to spread your fingers as much as you would have to on the C whistle. This
   is a great advantage to children, as it makes for more relaxed playing.
3. Traditional Irish music is mostly played in the key of D. The author wishes to thank Kevin
   Doherty A.R.A.M. for his advice and assistance in writing this book.

HOW TO PLAY THE TIN WHISTLE

NOTATION

- o These spots and circles represent the Tin Whistle.
- o The spots indicate the fingers to be placed on the whistle.
- o The circles indicate the holes to be left open.
- ●
- ●
- ●

A half filled circle ─◐─ represents a half-tone. The finger should be placed on the top half o the hole only.

- + This cross indicates that the note is played in the upper octave. This may be obtained b blowing somewhat stronger.

 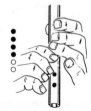 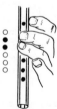

NOTES ON THE TIN WHISTLE

KEY OF D

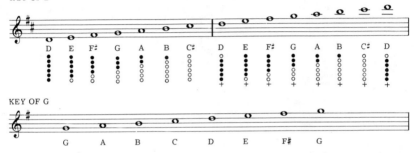

KEY OF G

The note of C Natural (C♮) on the D whistle may be fingered in the three following ways:

THE TIN WHISTLE

HOLDING

The tin whistle rests on both thumbs, which are placed underneath. The little fingers which are not used for playing notes are placed on either side.

   IMPORTANT : Always make sure that the holes that are stopped (this means covered or closed) are completely covered.

BLOWING

Notes are produced by blowing through the mouthpiece. Two notes may be obtained from the same hole.

To get the notes on the lower octave you only need to breathe or blow gently through the mouthpiece.

The notes on the upper octave may be obtained by blowing somewhat stronger. In either case it is important to maintain a steady air flow.

RUDIMENTS OF MUSIC

Music is written by means of signs or symbols, called notation after the first seven letters of the alphabet:

A B C D E F G

These notes are written on five horizontal lines and between four spaces called the STAVE or STAFF.

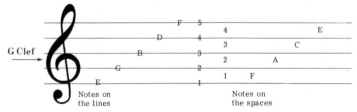

G Clef

Notes on the lines

Notes on the spaces

Note: It is important to memorise the position of these notes. The notes on the lines may be learned more easily by memorising the following:

<u>E</u>very <u>G</u>ood <u>B</u>oy <u>D</u>eserves <u>F</u>avours

and the space notes - F A C E (face)

6

LEGER NOTES are an extension of the staff. These are
short horizontal lines which are placed above and below
the stave when required. Below is an example of leger
notes written thus:

	Leger	3	D	Leger	3	E
	spaces	2	B	spaces	2	C
	above	1	G	above	1	A

	Leger	1	D	Leger	1	C	MIDDLE C
	spaces	2	B	spaces	2	A	
	below	3	G	below	3	F	

BAR LINES

Music is divided into equal periods of time by means of Bar Lines.

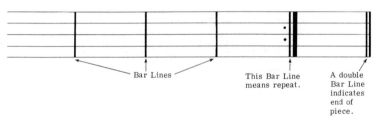

Bar Lines

This Bar Line means repeat.

A double Bar Line indicates end of piece.

TIME SIGNATURES

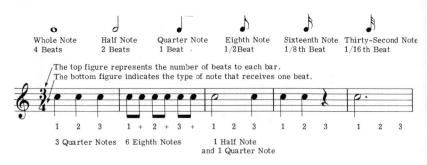

The top figure represents the number of beats to each bar.
The bottom figure indicates the type of note that receives one beat.

You will note in the above example that while there is a
varied number of notes to each bar, their total number
of beats or counts invariably amount to three.

A dot placed after a note increases its value by half. 𝅗𝅥.

VIBRATO

This quivering effect on the notes may be obtained by tapping rapidly on the whistle.

For example; for the note of G tap rapidly on the F♯ hole.

 ←—— Tap rapidly on this hole.

This method is very effective when playing slow airs.

ROLLING

This method is used by most of the Irish Players. It is quite difficult to learn but once mastered proves well worth the effort.

The last four notes which are joined together are played very quickly with a reflex action.

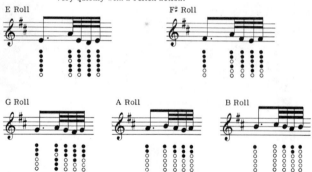

COCKLES AND MUSSELS

THE WILD ROVER

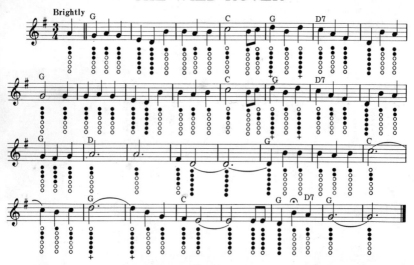

THE MERRY PLOUGHBOY

THE LONDONDERRY AIR (Danny Boy)

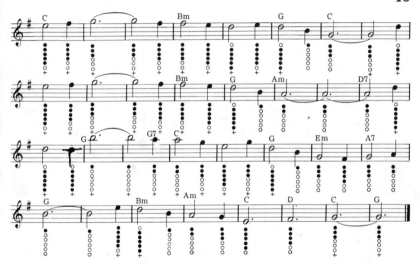

THE BOYS OF BLUEHILL

Bright with spirit

Hornpipe

THE FOGGY DEW

DUMPHY'S HORNPIPE

Hornpipe

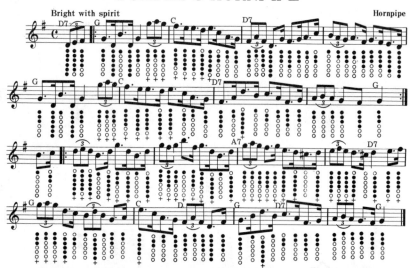

THE OLD WOMAN FROM WEXFORD

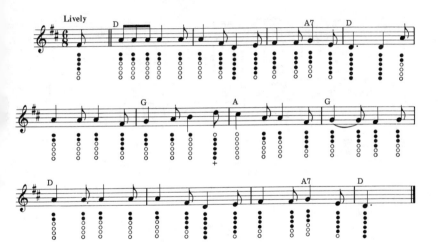

THE HARVEST HOME

Bright with spirit

Hornpipe

THE SALLY GARDENS

THE LIVERPOOL HORNPIPE

Bright with spirit

Hornpipe

THE ROCKY ROAD TO DUBLIN

THE BUTCHER BOY

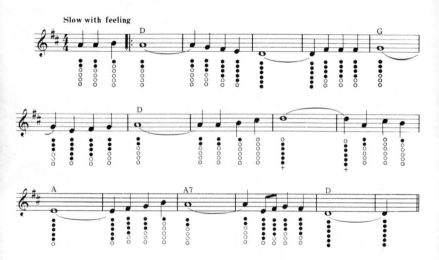

SAINT PATRICK'S DAY

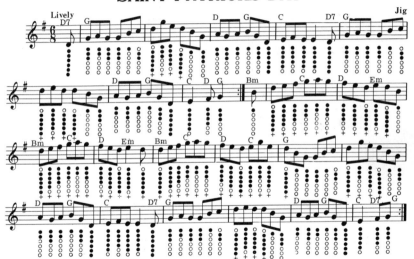

LOVE IS TEASIN'

THE RAKES OF MALLOW

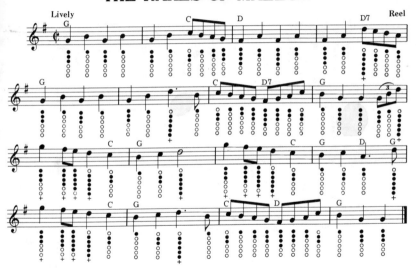

THE IRISH WASHERWOMAN

HASTE TO THE WEDDING

DROWSY MAGGIE

Reel

MISS MCLEOD'S REEL

THE GALWAY RACES

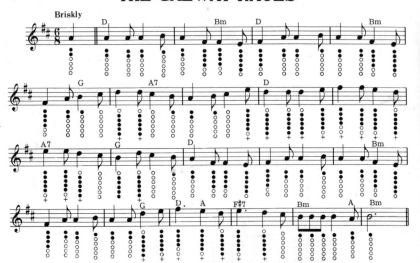